A Ho Nellie

By Cynthia Benjamin

Illustrated by Jan Palmer

CELEBRATION PRESS

Pearson Learning Group

Contents

Characters

Josh Jamison . . . . 10 years old

Ana . . . . 10 years old

Mrs. Jamison . . . . Josh's mother

Sam . . . . 10 years old

Mr. Lee . . . . apartment superintendent

Ms. Lopez . . . . a fourth-grade teacher

Mr. Frank . . . . director of the Greene
Street Community Center

Mr. and Mrs. Ryan . . . community center visitors

Nellie . . . . a terrier-like dog

Extras . . . . other fourth grade students and
senior citizens

Act 1 Scene I

The present; late afternoon, behind an apartment building where Josh and Ana are practicing baseball and the dog Nellie is watching them.

ANA: *(batting)* I'm glad your family moved here. You're the best pitcher we've ever had.

JOSH: Thanks. I like it here okay, but it would be much better if I could have a dog.

ANA: Oh, Josh, not that again!

JOSH: *(shrugging)* I like dogs, and dogs like me. Watch. *(whistles to dog)* Here, Nellie!

(Josh kneels and pets the dog while Ana watches him.)

ANA: How do you know her name?

JOSH: We're old friends. You know the bookstore on Third Avenue? Mr. Marks, the owner, told me he found her out back when he bought the place two years ago. He feeds her and lets her sleep in the store.

ANA: Wait. Didn't that place close?

JOSH: *(looking shocked)* What? The bookstore?

ANA: Yes. Josh, I think your friend Nellie may be homeless.

Scene II

Early evening. Ana and Josh walk down a city street.

ANA: *(pointing to store and dog)* Look! The bookstore *is* closed. I wonder where Mr. Marks has gone.

JOSH: And I wonder where Nellie is going to find a new home.

ANA: Not in our apartment building. That's for sure.

JOSH: Let's stop at the grocery store. We need to get some dog food.

ANA: Are you trying to drag me into some kind of plan to save Nellie?

JOSH: What if I was?

ANA: Nothing. I love dogs, just like you do.

JOSH: Good. I may need help.

ANA: Josh, if you are thinking of keeping Nellie, forget it. No way are dogs allowed in our building.

JOSH: *(whistles innocently)*

ANA: Josh, I mean it. Tenants in our apartment building can't have pets.

JOSH: But we can't put a poor homeless dog out on the street! Suppose my mom says I can keep her? What's the worst thing that could possibly happen?

ANA: You'd have to move in 30 days.

Scene III

After dinner, outside the apartment building in a small storage shed. Ana and Josh are drying Nellie after the dog's bath. Ana and Josh are both pretty wet.

ANA: I'm soaked. Why didn't you tell me that dogs shake out their coats like that after a bath?

JOSH: To be honest, I didn't know. *(to Nellie)* Wasn't that a great bath, girl? *(to Ana)* Anyway, it was your bright idea.

ANA: Not exactly. All I said was, "This dog probably overturned a garbage can."

JOSH: Then you should have just held your nose or something. Now that she's dry, we can feed her.

ANA: *(holds up a can opener)* I already thought of that.

JOSH: Thanks, Ana. You're a real pal.

(Mrs. Jamison enters, carrying a blanket and a pillow.)

MRS. JAMISON: How's it going in here?

ANA: Fine, Mrs. Jamison.

JOSH: We've got everything under control. Stop worrying, Mom.

MRS. JAMISON: How can I not worry? I said you could keep Nellie here in the shed, but I don't know what the building manager will say when he gets back. If only Mr. Lee hadn't gone on vacation ...

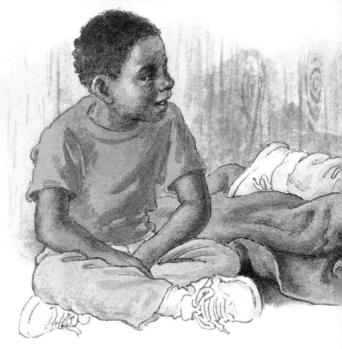

JOSH: Mom, it's no big deal.

MRS. JAMISON: No, Josh, you're wrong. It *is* a big deal. I wish Mr. Lee were here. I'm sure he won't mind if Nellie stays here just this one night, but I'd feel better if I'd been able to ask him ahead of time.

JOSH: What are the blanket and pillow for?

MRS. JAMISON: Oh, I brought these for Nellie.

JOSH: *(with a huge smile)* Thanks, Mom!

MRS. JAMISON: Remember what I said, though. This is just for tonight.

(*Mrs. Jamison leaves.*)

JOSH: Now I'm the one who's worrying. Nellie needs a place to stay...by tomorrow night!

ANA: Don't worry, Josh. We'll think of something.

JOSH: I sure hope so.

END OF ACT I

Act 2 Scene I

The next morning, in Ana and Josh's classroom. The fourth-grade students are seated at their desks. Their teacher, Ms. Lopez, stands at the front.

MS. LOPEZ: Class, remember this Friday we leave for the Greene Street Community Center at nine o'clock. We'll spend the morning there before returning to school. Now, who can tell us about the community center? *(Sam raises his hand.)*

JOSH: *(whispers to Ana)* Sure. It figures that know-it-all Sam has the answer.

ANA: I know what you mean.

SAM: *(proudly)* The Greene Street Community Center offers activities and special classes for senior citizens. Sometimes there are special events and speakers, too.

MS. LOPEZ: Thank you, Sam. That was very helpful. Does anyone have any questions?

ANA: What about our group projects?

MS. LOPEZ: I'm glad you asked, Ana. I want groups of three or four students to work together to prepare reports about different kinds of community services. Also, explain what your group might do to help our community. *(Suddenly a dog barks outside. Ana looks at Josh, and he starts to cough as if trying to cover the sound of the dog.)* Josh, are you okay?

JOSH: *(coughing)* I'm fine, Ms. Lopez. I must have an allergy or something.

SAM: *(whispering to Ana)* Maybe he's allergic to dogs. *(Ana glares at him.)*

MS. LOPEZ: I want the names of the students in each group by Friday. *(The lunch bell rings.)* We'll talk more about our projects tomorrow. See you after lunch.

(As class files out, Josh and Ana look out the window.)

JOSH: *(pointing)* Look, it's Nellie. She followed us to school.

The school cafeteria. Josh and Ana are eating lunch.

ANA: How did she get out? Didn't you lock the door?

JOSH: *(embarrassed)* Not exactly. I just hated the idea of Nellie being cooped up all day in that little shed. So I left the door open a crack after I walked her this morning.

ANA: Josh, someone could have seen Nellie and had her sent to the pound!

JOSH: *(looking worried)* We have to find a place for Nellie fast!

(Sam walks over and sits down next to Josh.)

SAM: Is it okay if I join you?

JOSH: Sure.

ANA: *(sweetly)* I have one condition. May I *please* have your extra hamburger?

SAM: *(suspiciously)* Okay, that does it. What's up, you guys?

JOSH: *(smiling slyly at Ana)* Why nothing. We're just trying to be friendly, that's all.

SAM: You two? That's a laugh. *(hands Ana hamburger)* Still, anything for a friend.

ANA: Thanks.

SAM: Now that we're friends, though, you have to be honest with me.

ANA: About what?

SAM: *(holding up fingers)* Number one: A strange dog barks outside our classroom. Number two: Josh's coughing was a cover-up. Number three: Ana doesn't even like hamburgers! So tell me, guys, what's going on? *(Josh and Ana look at each other.)*

Scene III

After school in the storage shed. Josh, Ana, and Sam are playing with Nellie.

SAM: *(petting Nellie)* Wow, she's an incredible dog. I can't believe how well-trained she is. *(Josh and Ana look at each other, surprised.)*

JOSH: There's more to you than I thought, Sam. I never realized you were a dog person.

SAM: I am, in a major way. There's only one small problem. *(He sneezes.)* I'm allergic to them. They make me sneeze. *(He sneezes again.)*

ANA: *(hands him a tissue)* Here.

SAM: Thanks. I think it's great that the two of you are taking care of Nellie, but why is she staying here in the storage shed?

JOSH: That's a long story.

SAM: Are your parents allergic or something?

JOSH: *(looking at Ana)* Not exactly. It's more like a difference of opinion.

ANA: I'll translate that. Josh wants to keep
Nellie, but it's against the rules. Tenants
can't have pets in our building.

SAM: Now I get it.

JOSH: *(quickly)* So we need to find a home
for Nellie. Fast.

SAM: *(nodding)* That's great. What's your plan?

JOSH: *(nervously)* We don't have one yet. Do
you have any ideas?

SAM: My mom's a vet, so I know a lot about dogs. Maybe we can figure this out.

JOSH: Deal.

ANA: This could be the beginning of a beautiful friendship.

SAM: To quote my mom, "A dog isn't a toy." That's another way of saying that Nellie needs a lot of care.

JOSH: Tell me about it. I had to walk her at six o'clock this morning.

SAM: Be realistic, guys. Nellie can't stay here forever.

JOSH: We know. She can't even stay here tonight.

(Mr. Lee enters, sees dog, and stops, hands on hips.)

MR. LEE: You've got that right. Can someone please tell me what this dog is doing in here?

END OF ACT II

Act 3 Scene I

A few minutes later in the superintendent's office. Mr. Lee is leaning on his desk. He looks sternly at Josh, Sam, and Nellie. Nellie's head is down.

JOSH: We can explain everything, sir.

SAM: This dog's owner abandoned her.

JOSH: Yes, and we...we rescued her!

(Mrs. Jamison and Ana enter.)

MRS. JAMISON: I'm sorry, Mr. Lee. I didn't know what to do, so I told Josh he could keep Nellie in the shed for one night. I planned to ask you if it would be okay, but then I found out you were away.

MR. LEE: That's right. My first vacation in two years, but I had to come back early. *(clears throat)* Now, about this dog... *(He reaches down to scratch Nellie behind the ears. She responds by jumping into his lap.)* Whoa. I think she likes me.

MRS. JAMISON: We'll get her out of here right away, Mr. Lee. It's just that Josh has always wanted a dog. When he realized Nellie was homeless, he just had to help her.

MR. LEE: I don't make the rules, Josh. If it was up to me, I'd let you keep her. The problem is. . .

ANA, JOSH, SAM: *(together)* . . . tenants can't have dogs in this building.

JOSH: I think it's a rotten rule!

MR. LEE: I agree. But it *is* the rule.

JOSH: It's just not fair. Nellie *needs* a home.

MR. LEE: *(sighs)* Okay, here's what I'll do. Nellie can stay in the shed for two more days. Then she'll have to go.

JOSH: Thanks, Mr. Lee!

MRS. JAMISON: Now let's get this dog out of Mr. Lee's office. *(Mrs. Jamison, Josh, Ana, Sam, and Nellie leave the office.)*

JOSH: Now we really do have a problem.

ANA: Actually, we have two. The first one is Nellie. The second is our class project.

SAM: *(snapping his fingers)* And I think I can solve both of them, with a little help from my mom and Ms. Lopez, of course.

Scene II

Two days later, in Ana, Josh, and Sam's classroom. Ana, Josh, and Sam are standing in front of the class. Ms. Lopez is talking to the students.

MS. LOPEZ: Now the next group of students will talk about their community service project. When they're finished, we have a special visitor to introduce to the class.

JOSH: *(stepping forward)* Sam and Ana and I are doing a project about how dogs help people feel better. Sam's mom is a vet, and she told him about these special programs in hospitals so dogs can visit patients there.

SAM: *(stepping forward)* Thank you, Josh. I do know a lot about the subject.

JOSH: *(softly, to Ana)* Oh, no, the know-it-all is back.

SAM: *(to Ana and Josh)* Well, what I mean is that the *three* of us have done some research on these programs.

MS. LOPEZ: *(to Sam)* Remember, Sam, our special visitor is waiting patiently outside in the hallway.

SAM: *(to the class)* Doctors have discovered that just petting a dog can make a person feel happier and more relaxed.

ANA: *(to the class)* Doctors test their patients' heartbeats before and after petting a dog. After petting a dog for a while, some people's heartbeats actually slow down.

JOSH: What we're trying to say is that dogs are actually good for your health. It's a cool idea, when you think about it. *(A dog barks in the hallway. The students look around excitedly.)*

MS. LOPEZ: I think it's time to introduce our special visitor. *(Ms. Lopez leaves the classroom for a few seconds. When she returns, she's holding Nellie's leash. The students clap.)*

JOSH: *(taking Nellie's leash)* This is Nellie. I guess she's the most important part of our project. She's a pretty terrific dog, too.

ANA: *(smiling)* It's a really long story, but we'll tell you all about it when we get to the community center.

SAM: I think we have time to explain it now. *(Nellie barks; the students laugh.)* Okay, okay, we'll wait until we get to the community center.

Scene III

Ms. Lopez, her class, Mr. Frank, and some senior citizens are in the Greene Street Community Center. Nellie stands next to Ana, Josh, and Sam.

MR. FRANK: *(smiling)* I'd like to welcome the students from Ms. Lopez's class to our community center. We always enjoy having visitors, and today we have a special one. *(Nellie barks.)*

MS. LOPEZ: I'd like to introduce Nellie to everyone here at the center. She's going to be helping you, but she's also going to be helping some of my students.

ANA: Mr. Frank has agreed to let Nellie stay here at the center. She's really friendly and loves people. *(to Josh)* You tell the rest.

JOSH: After Nellie was abandoned, we needed to find a home for her. When we talked to Mr. Frank, he offered to adopt her. *(Everyone claps.)*

SAM: (*stepping forward*) Of course, we still have to do our class project. So our group will visit the Greene Street Community Center once a week for the next month. We'll give Nellie a bath and help introduce her to the seniors who come here. Then we're going to see how well Nellie gets along with all the visitors here. Later we'll write a report and present it in class.

JOSH: We think it will be a great project for us, for Nellie, and for the community center.

MR. RYAN: On behalf of all of us here at the center, I'd like to thank you. We're going to love having Nellie here with us.

MRS. RYAN: *(petting Nellie)* I can't think of a better friend to join our group. Now, what do you think of all this attention, Nellie?

(Nellie barks.) (Josh leans down to hug Nellie.)

JOSH: See, I told you it would all work out.

THE END